In Praise of Thought

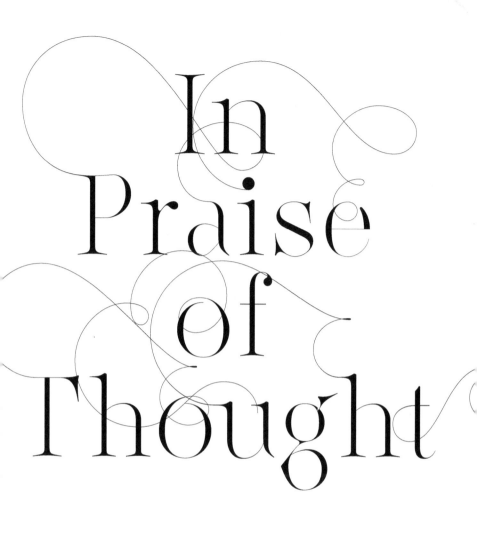

haddad books

In Praise of Thought

Elizabeth Haddad

A Note

In Praise of Thought is a collection of poetry about identity, place, human connection, and the internet.

These poems were written over a period of seven years. It began as a way of processing. Around 2013, it was evident that human interaction had changed irrevocably. Of course, the internet was in our lives long before, but, as the second decade of a new millennium unfolded, to *be* became mostly virtual.

The platforms we now call *social media* have effectively infiltrated every aspect of our lives, and, with them, an industry of information and consumption has rapidly institutionalized.

The origins of our web are arguably troubling. A few individuals (mostly male, mostly white) were afforded an epic responsibility: the ability to make astronomical decisions about society through the building of apps, with little oversight. They were able to determine the ways in which we exist and relate to one another (*content, likes*) and how we communicate with each other (*texts, comments*), all the while preying on and profiting from our behavior (*ads, cookies, data collection*).

Through these apps, we have built ourselves into a virtual society with little pushback or questioning of whether these parameters are accurate reflections of ourselves as complete beings. Our online lives and our tangible, vibrant ones have become so entangled, they are difficult to separate. It is nearly impossible to exist outside these virtual structures. It all feels terribly existential.

Early on, I participated heavily in crafting an online identity. I yearned to build a career as a writer, which required me to build myself as a persona. In time, I became exhausted with my virtual self: the upkeep consumed me, left me feeling empty, required me to brand the most sacred parts of me—my body, my ideas, my time. Not to mention the sheer fatigue that came from an unrelenting stream of imagery, information, and opinion.

These poems reflect that disillusion. Still, I can't ignore that many have used these apps as tools for profound good. The internet, in essence, serves a great purpose: its existence provides us the opportunity to disseminate and democratize information, forces us to reckon with the many grim realities that exist within society. It has often served me a humbling education.

In my fantasy, empathy and privacy would have been built into the foundations of our internet; third-party services would never be allowed to manipulate thought and behavior through algorithm; apps would not be designed to consume our time and addict our brains; and it would be unethical, if not illegal, for companies to use surveillance and data collection to make money off our thoughts, voices, and bodies.

More than ever, we are being forced to confront who we are, *what* we are, and whether *this* internet is the neutral tool we believe it to be. *In Praise of Thought* digs into the flesh of these existential questions. These poems are an attempt to examine our internet, but, more acutely, they are a meditation on what makes us alive.

What does it mean to be human? I turned almost religiously to the concept of duality. I wanted to examine the dualities that coexist in society and within the self. Ultimately, I searched for grounding in the idea of home: Are we at home in one particular place, or can we find home within? I returned to my own West Virginian *state of being.*

I hoped to give these questions greater context than the internet would ever allow while also giving duality to the internet itself. Poetry allowed me to express the existential most accurately because the medium, in essence, is abstract; each word in a poem is conscious and weighted, yet much is often left between the lines.

In the end, we build our technologies and thus hold the power to change them. As the internet evolves, we must continuously query, through thought, criticism, poetry, and law: Is this technology functioning *for* us? And can a machine ever hold our fullness anyway?

Elizabeth Haddad

In

Praise

F

of

hought

How elegant a pause,
how swift a revelation.

How tender a reflection,
a moment steeped in awe.

This is a manifesto
in praise of the rational,
dreams analyzed
and obtained.

In praise of thought:
a reaction most mundane.

One should think:

when a foot hovers a curb,
as a finger caresses a button;

before an eye strays
or the hand lingers;

when angry or
intrigued;

while speaking to a friend
or dialing a lover;

before opening the door
to get in;

before leaving things
unsaid,
before saying anything at all;

while gazing out the window,
before opening the app;

when listening,
while talking,
when walking,
sitting,
as being;

prior to taking
or giving,
assuming and believing.

A moment of thought can:

mitigate a war;
clot blood before it spills;
suck up a bullet like a vacuum
cleaner.

A second of pause can
piece together another's reputation,
right before it hits the floor and shatters in
a hundred or more pieces.

Then there's the slow-burning kind,
the ilk of the daydreamer,
Rodin's bronzed man:
while sitting on the subway
or park bench,
when waiting in lines and
airport terminals
or doctors' offices.

The ever-incandescent right of the living
to discover and plot and navigate.

All without need of a humble fingertip,
and its
swiping
and scrolling
and opening
and closing,
or laughing
or degrading
or loving
or hating.

The rolling lull!
The heavy mundane!
The sparkling boredom
that sees a face unconsumed by
blue light.

The humble act of thought:
a true nectar of life.

Semanti

C,

Barrier

To be *of* life
is not to be life.

To be created *from* the sea
is not to be the sea:
that is to be strength.

To be *in* the clouds
is not to be the clouds:
that is to be freedom.

Such a small thing can so far remove.
> *To be as,*
> *to become,*
> *to be from,*
> *in or within.*

Imagine a single word, *of,*
a preposition
with power to determine an entire
existence.

For the self itself is of a permanent *of* –
one can only ever be of another,
perhaps from another,
yet one can never be another.

How we yearn to sink beneath another's skin,
beyond the skull,
to inhabit another's impassable mind.

To be known of
is to ensure one is never known.
You see one of a history
yet you cannot see history as one,
or one's history as your own.

One cannot be reborn
if one is seen only of certain birth –
that is to say of culture,
or eye color,
or the shape of one's nose.

I myself am everything,
though I am not made of everything.

You remain king of the earth
while you have difficulty becoming the earth
(dust to dust we all shall return).

Beyond the physical, what is the spirit of?
To be of religion is to write the book,
to be religion is to enter into divinity itself,
which has no words or pages
or spines.

To be of anything is to arm oneself:
a shield of protection,
a sword of distance.

Let language fall
from my tongue, evaporate.
It holds power, but
I need sentience.

Lead me to the edge,
crack my ribs open,
skull and heart split
to receive.

Watch as earth seeps inside until it becomes me
and I, earth.
I will be,

not a matter of consequence.

What's a Lan

in

guage ?

1.
What's in a language?
Say *skeleton* enough times –
say it one hundred times
and it becomes nothing more
than hard sounds beating
together.

Skeleton
skeleton
skeleton
skeleton
skeleton.

I remember when conversation
was our sole tether.
You'd call and we'd talk.
Our folded hours, you, my storyteller.
Your breath, my laugh.
All the vivid ways the world took us
in.

The world seemed bigger still,
your potential held everything
imaginable in me.

We would read and we would talk,
we talked about what we read.
We wanted to drink up everyone else
to broaden our own bodies of water.

2.
Now as you type LOL,
are you laughing?
How could I know?

A video, grainy, untouchable:
Is that any different than a secondhand voice,
crackling, sizzling through metal lines?

When you texted, *"I'm crying!"* I wished you were.
When you said, *"I'M DEAD!"* I wept for you.

Say *life* enough times,
and it becomes nothing more than
a collection of noise.

Life
life
life
life
life.

3.
I watch as my own body degrades
into pixels.
I disseminate around the world
and back again,
as the earth circles the sun;
countless fingers touch.

Another day will surely rise.
I fear not death, but illusion;
digital imprint immortal.

Why do we love to see, and see, and see some more?
Why do we love to look so many times, we lose sight?

Why,
do we

take another picture?

4.
Zoom in.
Regard my nose and eyes and
stray eyebrow hairs.

I am unsure of the reflection, so I take another,
and another,
and another,
and another,
so I can begin the process of curating
what remains.

Stare at the phone to gather receipt.
They will come
to deposit love,
words and phrases
repeated over
and over
and over
and over.
Say *love* enough times –
say it a hundred times – and it becomes
nothing.

Love
love
love
love
love.

But for a moment I will manifest.
And I will have no choice but to do it again
and again
and again
and again.

Because after that,
*c'est la meme
chose.*

to

Mariah

Cherubic face lit of soft
color.
Almond eyes, brightening
a television screen.
Hark! This tender-smiled
goddess.

Long and lean,
draped in black
velvet.

It was somewhere near '96.
I stood lost in:
a cloud of reverie;
        ominously hovering;
                envelops me;
        rhapsodize –

What peculiar words
she molded into melody.
Syllables trickling down
in rhythmic rain.
*(Keats and Frost were good but
this rang deep!)*

What a peculiar
little soul. I,
barely a decade alive,
hypnotized by the lulling
roll of her cassette tape –
rounding sound into
portal, I drifted in.

Her words stretched
from my young, green
tongue.

So soft and so sweet:
"Me and Mariah,
go back like babies and
pacifiers."

I was yet a tender child,
pale and olive unless
sun-touched.

Just a little ethnic,
just like Mariah –
not enough but almost
too much.
(A particular plight of the
quartered child.)

"It's hard to explain,
inherently it's just always
been strange,
neither here nor there."

Honeyed voice,
honey-streaked curls,
crafting worlds, enchanted.

"So starry eyed,
on the flowery hillside.
Breathless and fervid
amid the dandelions,"
she poured,
vibrato.

But what language was this!

A door swept open
unhinged in phrase,

"To just walk away from
the one thing that's
unyielding and sacred to me."

A young epiphany in hymn!
Words house their own spirit,
can be twisted into the meaning
I so desperately longed to
express.

"She smiles through a thousand
tears, and harbors adolescent fears,"

I sang, silent –
barely touching an
adolescence of my own –
to the apparition of my
middle school bully.

"Somewhere halfway,
feeling there's no one
completely the same,"

I wept in vast recognition,
tears dampening my basement
carpet in hallowed truth:
every child seeks
another to grasp them,
whole and beyond.

"And though time's rolled by,
still I feel like a child as I look at the moon.
Maybe I grew up a little too soon."

Yet her oracle spoke of more
than sight within.

Alas, vision
to become –

"Well here I am,
for all of them to bleed.
But they can't take my heart from me,
and they can't bring me to my knees!"

What an epic poet, Mariah!
Her art of song,
gifted from above;
all remedy found in the tone
of her voice.

An ode to Mariah:
my first love of the written
kind.

When We Talk about

the

Weather

"It's cold out there today!"
he said to me as I ambled out the door.
He and I speak almost every day.
Which is to say, he and I exchange pleasantries
about the weather.

I have often thought to myself:
Have we ever discussed anything else?
The answer is no. Nothing other than:
> *Sure is cold out!*
> *Can you believe this heat?*
> *It's raining again.*
> *Tomorrow shall be sunny!*

So today, as we have a hundred days before,
we spoke of the weather.
A sacred ritual, that which we share.

And I discovered something new!
He doesn't like this heat.
I tell him I do.
We part full of knowledge.

But in between words,
like *hot* and *cold,*
sun and *rain,*
spring and *fall,*
listen closely.
There beats something akin to Morse code,
thumping, spelling out:

Can you believe our luck?
You and I are here, floating through
the same air, faltering under
the same sky!

And also:
Can you fathom it?
Between us heavy
atmosphere opens, buoyant,
to infinity!
The space we gather reaches vastly,
for light years, stretching toward alien species,
away until it becomes something else's sky.

He and I are really talking math.
And by this equation, the universe and
its many galaxies, numbering
somewhere in the billions,
is simply one shared space.

Our earth is viewed by a galactic microbe
via microscope.
This very earth is a pinprick to Mars.
It's all one giant black

sea, punctured by energy, fire, light.
Unwavering infinity!
It's understandable that he and I would
have to calibrate language, simplify sounds
to express this ephemeral, eternal.

While he waxes about a sky cast in gray,
laments its relinquishing of cold rain –
truly, listen!
He's saying,
Look, there's no way of knowing
when all this will end.

And when he promises,
Tomorrow will be sunny!
The translation:

Tomorrow will come,
with or without us.

You see, our eyes have horizons
we cannot see past.
For Christ's sake, we are suspended in vastness!
We are overwhelmed,
we are nothing if not fleeting.

We can study philosophy, religion, and science.
We can widen the lens, but it's instinctive.
We must build walls to house ourselves in,
we crave warm wombs.

Floating boundless is pure angst.
We need ground.
We zoom in,
anchor in bodies,
eyelids and pores,
dead skin and bacteria.

We breathe out, crouch, bend forward,
fetal. We rest, so that the next time we attempt
to rise, to extend and discover what we really
are, we might find some peace.
With wisdom, we find that we are really

origami! Elastic, we stretch, reach,
boundless! Until we must
contract, fold, micro.
In this process, some few may
contract too much and too often,
break

off, and apart. Fractured, they may draw
lines between their bodies and
ours.

But there is always hope.
We are given space.
We can always look up, feel
the troposphere's movement
upon our skin,
humidity, wind, ice.

We can always inquire about the weather.
This inquiry holds faith *and* science.
It is energy.
It reverberates out and through
the universe.

It says:
We are here! You and I exist, together,
under the same eternal sky.

We breathe in,
a billion times infinity,

and then, we go.

Http://<404

Error>

(Human vs. Machine)

Recalculating. Recalculating.
The voice of God is nasal, shrill.
She's not as I expected.
Her voice reverberates,
fills space and void, bellows automatic.

She is nudging me toward redemption.
Recalculating. Recalculating. Reroute!

Whether it was I who was wrong,
or *she,* stands irrelevant.
(For the record: She won't update
autonomously.
Why does she refuse to grow?)
I breathe in sharply. I recall.
It's true that past follies are of universal order.

For example: some say *to err,*
<Error. Page not found> is to be a *problem.*
As if to *not err,* *<404>* is linked to virtue,
not beacon:
<404 Page not found. Refresh and try again.>

But to *not err* is suspect.
Artificial intelligence reads like insult.
Our human intellect waxes neurologic,
fires *au naturel.*

For example: our machine counterparts can
<Warning! Malfunction.>
They spark, electric; plugged in, deep
in computation; at ease in the transaction.
But alas, with only 99% accuracy,
they possess excessive room for error.

Our condition *to err* is not
some dead wire to extract,
but a root,
the motherboard of an essence.
We are all but inner children touching hot stoves.
*<Temperature! She needs to cool down
before you use her.>*

The computer logs her error in algorithm.
She is programmed to change course, according.
She rewires, reactive, efficient, quick!
But I want to know: *Did she even care?*

To be human is a far more just cause.
Humans suffer consequence.
With remorse, horizons of rising epiphanies appear.
A human holds innately her prospect
of suffering, of forgiveness
from another,
to another, to oneself.

The fallible human may drink from a
common human wound:
the bejeweled cup of misdeed.
Then, she may lather herself anew:
the healing sap of salvation.

To be alive is a problem.
We must proclaim again and again, with pain and triumph and
shame:

I am no error!
I err. I am alive. I recalculate.

Southern

Kitchen

Every week six women and one little
me would congregate around
the corner booth of an establishment called
Southern Kitchen.

Located on Maccorkle Avenue,
Southern Kitchen was beloved.
It lay deep within a neighborhood called
Kanawha City; one may ask how to pronounce
such a place, but I don't have time to explain –

Ancient Native American syllables flow from
hillbilly tongues as natural as words
like *"git"* and *"y'all,"*
and I think that amounts to something greater
but I can't be sure.

Southern Kitchen was alive, indefinitely.
It was decorated mostly brown,
flooded in warm fluorescent light.
It was known for the miniature ceramic chickens
lining its walls.
I loved the crinkle chips
and fried eggs with unnatural, sunflower-yellow yolk.

In the late evening, or early morn,
one could find the entire world:
paper-white cops inhaling eggs and toast
with grape jam next to
gruff rednecks fading into camouflage,
drag queens sipping coffee,
the young and the old,
Middle Eastern to Eastern Panhandle.

Later in life it was where
us Catholic school kids convened

at unspeakable hours, for a necessary meal of sponge
to soak up the evening's debacles.

It was a certain era:
my mother, a stylish '90s blonde,
Princess Di haircut,
designer suede boots
and sparkling blue eyes.
And friends:

A bobbed dark-blonde of
        dry wit and class;
A plump, nurturing Italian
        of sharp mind, who hugged deep;
A warm, diminutive Colombian
        who spoke furiously, comedic timing supreme;
A trim, tanned intellectual
        of cropped black hair and biting tongue;
A beautiful Cubana
        in bedazzled shoulder pads, booming voice
        and wild ringlets touching high and wide.

I want to paint a picture for you.
These six women held court
each week to speak a state of affairs.
To discuss a possible future.
To laugh and insult and validate.

Those early days, my mother
would invite six-year-old me
to sit amongst these women representing
God's creative will.

I filled my seat at the table, though I was too small
to see above the table's edge.
Sometimes I'd bring crayons to color,

a toy to occupy time.
Mostly, I watched and
I listened.

These six women hardly ever ordered food
(perhaps an omelet, some toast.)
But they *always* ordered coffee.
Six cups of coffee would arrive on a dirty black tray,
dense white mugs filled of liquid, lukewarm.

The women would begin to color their coffee:
one Sweet'N Low,
I prefer the blue packet,
two creamers,
one creamer,
she likes it black.

They held the cups intimately, like a child,
hands enveloping mug
so one couldn't separate body from ceramic.
I noticed as each woman took a first sip
of a fresh pour, it was like deep breathing,
a moment of ecstasy and serenity,
an elixir that gave birth.

They'd drink in between
laughs and stories, cups filled over and over
until minutes collapsed.
The laughter got louder,
the stories more wrong.
Half-moons of red and pink lips stained cup edges
like pointillist paintings.

I'd beg my mother for a sip.
She'd acquiesce.
I found the taste bitter but the warmth comforting.

I wondered how they all grew to love
something like that.
They'd laugh as I scrunched my face.

I asked for the bitter drink each time.
I'd force it down, bear it with grace,
until I learned to crave it.

I guess they really taught me how
to be a woman.

The
Th

I'm hanging on by a thread!
she told me.
I searched for the thread,
she searched for a pear.
We were at the grocery store
and she was standing upright.

It got me thinking.
Life is both fragile and persistent:
one for one, one for another.

A forty-foot drop and the contents of his head
are splayed out on the pavement;
he breathes yet.

A slight twist of the spine and her head fills of
more than it can handle and no release;
she breathes not.

It's precarious.
We often survive something we shouldn't
just to die of a fluke.

One could say it's funny,
but it's certainly
no joke.

It's an invisible measure –
some century-old dame
falls down the stairs and
shatters a brittle femur.
She has yet more years to ponder.

A cautious son is hit head-on by
a bad decision.
And that's that.

We are all dangling by a thread,
connected to what feels like whim.

Or for some of faith,
the thread is sewn on by design.

Is this thread titanium?
Or more like a strand
of human hair –
surprisingly resilient yet easily
snapped by two fingers,
quickly singed into debris
by sporadic flame?

Some thread refuses to break no
matter the peril.
Others are born already fractured,
as if the faintest of breaths could
blow them to pieces.

Who weaves each thread
to each body? And how
come so bare?

I'd prefer a blanket I could wrap
around and in.
Something heavy, weighted,
warm.

What kind of existence is this?
Always hanging on to dear life!

What faith could I clumsily grasp,
if only to relinquish control to
a line so delicate?

Oh well,
it's no matter.
The thread dangles,
we hold tight.

Or not.

It's what gives life
its punch.

A
West
Virginia
Stream

Welcome to West Virginia!
Disappear into this uneasy silence thick with
all that's ever been unsaid.

Atop this mountain
reaching deep into our chemical valley,
an unsung revelation:
the state of being
the most high and
the absolute low.

All Lebanese
and native,
blonde-haired
hillbilly.
So many trust fund babies
below the Mason-Dixon
and poverty lines.

Coal mining
lovers of earth
will always smile,
shaking one's hand,
not to be mistaken with the recognition
of an outsider's fables.

A Black Diamond crooner,
an Arab pack peddler –
this land speaks truth out on
a back road.

Slow conversation in the atrium
of a shopping mall.
Tabbouleh
and boiled green beans
with hot dogs

and moonshine
spread out onto the table
like fine china with plastic forks.

The highest and
most absolute low
in fact lie upon the same
longitude.

I go there myself to lie down in sparse grass,
within the crevice of a hill
where no one can find me.

I used to catch salamanders in the stream,
my father was a businessman.
We own the land
but the land owns us
and still we owe something in the end.
(Who seeded this ground before we?)

This love of land
isn't some platform,
it's birthed,
as we are, out of the union of
a mountaintop and its own father's destruction.

If everywhere else is the land of opportunity,
why does West Virginia feel more free?

Boone County wisdom,
Appalachian lilt –
my Arab lineage, knee-deep in water
as he follows the Little Coal River home.

A cup of French press coffee at a
franchised steakhouse:

the highest of highs and
the lowest of all states.

For once and for all,
not the western part of Virginia!
No geographical solution can separate from this
union.

So they ask:
How does one
pronounce West Virginia –
in Arabic,
in Hindi?

Quiet!
She speaks with the tree frogs
come dusk –

Such a pity
you, *outside,*
may never hear
her strange and beautiful
noise.

ntion

A hand can hold,
caress,
grip,
strangle;

give bread,
withhold,

starve when able.

A knife can cut:

rope,
tomatoes,
packages open.

A knife can gut:

a fish or
innocent flesh.

A spoon:
feed
or coddle,
add or take some
away.

A device can
crack open a mind,

or waste one.

New Age

Money.

Those boys taunt *nouveau riche,*
but I know where we come from
and they don't –

headlines and palms dyed black of coal grease,
spine steel strong,
pitched deep within someone else's graveyard.

Do we carry the dead's sacrifice?
Can we ever begin anew?

Giddee was new money and he knew it.
Gold chains and tanned skin and names called.
Orthodox Syrian Baptist Evangelist
without one God to pray to!
There was only one way to save a self.

But he and Najeeb believed that
with every dollar earned,
one goes into the people's jar and he
passed that down to his girls.

Build, they told us;
build for, with your people.

Lester believed in bacon and eggs fried in pork fat
in the mornings,
which killed him eventually but it's good advice
to start your mornings with a hearty breakfast.

In his case morning may be lit of hard moon,
all for some abstract premonition,
future geometric enclaves to crouch under and
crunch numbers.

Lawrence (of Arabia!) knew that a pile
of bills could be torched
into paper trails but a stack of bricks
is a bit harder to dismantle.
Larry also knew that good businesswomen were
gentle sharks by nature,
but you boys bark like seals
and assume we can hear you.

New money becomes old money at some point.
New age becomes old as we leave earth
gasping our name.
Someone else had to work from the ground up
so their namesake could be born upon the peak.

There's no shame in money,
only the way it stains your skin
green, which doesn't bring you closer
to God's green earth but further away –
imagine a piece of paper's fate in a typhoon.

There's no shame in where you come from,
if you recall the way and stay the course
and only peer backward
to salute a trail of exhausted mothers.

There's no shame in any of it
as long as I know
I was only meant to add a mile,

fresh dust on a child's highway.

God Made the Mind

(The
Mind
Is
God)

I miss being blind to truth. *It's funny to enunciate the sin*. It may have been wrong, but damn was it warm

inside buoyant white taffeta, delicate flower crown entangling coarse waves. The code of attire was

gorgeous! He must have eyed us up and down in glory. I miss being seen. I don't miss being seen and

unheard. I miss hope, access to God within a man's contrition. I miss contrary forces resting together

without study, eye to eye without sense. I miss how things didn't require a sense. I lost my religion.

And with it, everything good. Somehow, the sinning stuck, like pockmarks, circular, pathologic,

and whole. I hold tight to fear and turmoil, what impressive guilt! I allowed good faith and high

redemption to dissolve into breath, too fragile to swallow. Man's shame made root and burrowed

deep, a seedling strong with neither source nor light. *(I tend to it dearly, out of habit.)* Shame is the fragrant

mint in a church's forest. I do miss the congregation, the holiness of another's voice singing me into their

sanctuary. Even when they mocked, there was purity in being bound to another. I do miss the ease of one

word. I kept the doubt. It was ever-present, no antagonist to faith but its companion, undying.

Conviction! What small penance to pay for certainty,
for sight beyond. I yearn to live again. Instead, I grow

to accept the sanctity of an hour, have faith in
my own resign. I mourn for religion. And thus, the

comfort of a distant shore. Uncertain yet, I open wide,
to drink from this sea: so unrelenting; I float in these

currents: so unbound. (*What tantalizing, brutal
depths!*) Alas, I turn to God – She, so holy! She,

most precious and good. She, who transcends
all with her most terrifying, valiant creation:

this sublime,
most divine mind.

My
Fantasy,

My Privacy

1.
Take record of it.
I, take record of.
I press record,
record every angle of my
face –
yet still I cannot see.

2.
In my fantasy I am free
from records.
I wipe birth certificates clean,
cannot find a phone number
or previous address.

In this dream, I shatter
any glass that holds too
tightly onto reflection.

One should not hoard material things;
material things should not hoard
what was intended
to be transient.

3.
As a young girl I traced
my imprint onto the soft dirt
of our World,
Wide Web –
folly and triumph,
equal.

I imagined earth as good,
Its people, solid.
I foresaw woman, man and child
extending elegant, interlocked fingers

long and far to catch me in their
web,

world widening.
Woven to widen our world.
To connect us by delicate silken
thread, so thin and clear,
nearly imperceptible
until it catches the light,
glistening in our man-made sun.

4.
Now I wish to scrub all
imprint away. I find
my own path impermeable. Made by me
but not for me.

After all, an imprint is
a thing and a thing
is not a person and
a person is not the imprint
left behind but the matter itself!

*I send a grounding prayer into the
universe.*

5.
She takes a picture of the web,
geometry dancing over
and again.

The web's weaver remains hidden,
small beneath rock and
dark crevice,
they enjoy shadow.

Their message, nonetheless, she knows.
She must record sight.
All that remains of sight is the record of it.
She gently presses
record.

6.
My fantasy, my privacy.
My privacy, anonymity.

My dreams overflow
with private strolls and
private chaos, disappearing
texts
and untracked trails,
tête-à-têtes and eyes
to eyes,
memory memorialized in my mind
alone,
what's mine is mine and
what's yours is yours,
what's just for me,
never for you to see!

7.
Your fantasy,
my privacy.

Your world,
our ears to
the public;
one billion eyes
switched on in the
living room;
hearts beating to
5G.

Your fantasy,
your innovation,
your connection,
our thoughts:
watch as we livestream
our own massacre.

8.
My only hope:
what bled in
the darkness
shall clot, become whole
in all-encompassing
light.

Everyone looks.

But remember:
nothing is gained
without something
given.

Don't forget the ones
who made us pay
for all the good this has
caused.

Everything,

All at Once

I close my eyes to summon the world.
It fits snug within the soft tissue
of a quiet, gentle mind.

I linger there; I take my time.
Water the jungles in salt,
test polarities in the body's circuitry.
I grow flushed with beauty:

The curvature of an earthly face,
the hue of an earthly skin,
the fluidity of a galloping bone,
a flush of blood recoloring pinched flesh!

I see we cannot float away,
we are magnetized.

And suddenly, at the very same instant,
upon the very same time,
this *very same world*
thrusts me back, *repels*.

I can no longer embody,
nor wrap myself around.
I may only peer through
from great distance,
eyes pried open in force.

What rotundness, how overbearing!
What depth of darkness, *unhinged*.
There is no gentle mind,
I fall without grasp.

The world is like this:
Wrought and wrung out,
circling for prey, tilted

only slightly in madness,
tickling unfathomable pain,
a fat bowl of waste.

The world is like this:
A sensual graze, a tender kiss,
pursed lips, cold
water rushing over burnt skin,
a forgotten granule of sugar
found on the tongue,
a sudden lick of sweetness,
a sudden peace.

Everything, all at once.

Love likes to sidle up,
take a seat, intermingle with
an urge to maim,
a call to kill, our collective,
primordial yearn
to hurt and humiliate.

We are capable of casting out humans
as if a body can be trash,
as if something alive could ever disappear.
We can be beautiful.

But one thing *in* is not
necessarily another *out.*
One thing added, is not
necessarily another taken away.
Nothing negates nothing.

Lock him away and he persists –
out of sight, out of mind,
but never out of world.

And upon death, a body may disintegrate
with time, or be burnt into instant dust.
Still, molecules disperse from the ash to take
their place inside another's breath.
Still, we cannot float away.

There are seasons, yes,
but there are universals:
hot and cold, joy and sadness,
wet and dry, war and peace.

Goodness does not allow rest,
and evil does not require
a constant cloak of despair.

There are good humans, yes,
but there are bad who get right,
and good who have been wronged,
and yet good who may do the wronging again.

I don't mean to summon all cliché,
but wrapped up in one tiny nanosecond
is everything.

Everything, all at once.

A first breath, a last exhale –
Official Time of Birth for he,
Official Time of Death for she,
one's ectasy,
one's anguish,
in one minute.

It's happening half a globe away,
on another continent,
in another soul,

within the same city,
under the same roof,
inside one body.

Everything is happening all
at one time, the entire breadth of
it, and yet, nothing is negated or lessened,
few are greater because.

Another's rise will never heal another's pain;
it can only assure that height exists.
Another's fall will never lift another's step;
it can only instruct how the ground swallows whole.

The world is like this:
Everything existing,
all at one time –
to everyone, to someone,
to you, to all.

The world should be taken like this:
Everything, all at once.

Ro

Rome,
eternal in my mind.

Eternally cased in ethereal gold light.

A gilded, kingly place, though
I'm struck by its chaotic gentleness.
A maternal city Rome remains.

No other stone holds these many spirits,
this dustiness of ash —

the remains of Caesar,
of Hadrian,
of the enslaved who birthed freedom,
of the powerful women
who wrote history in their name.

The overgrown banks of the Tiber
are of the most obscure beauty.
They allot a profound breeze,
as the spirits lie down out of breath
in attempt to cleanse you of
your own country.

After a while in Rome,
you give in,
collapsing into its
crumbled matter.

How freeing it is to glide through the air
as holy ash in the sky.

How noble it is to billow
with the gold dust
of Rome.

Acknowle

dgments

This book is indebted to many. *It takes a village.*

To all the poets whose work provided me with an informal education (the best kind) and from whom I took endless inspiration, most notably:

Pablo Neruda, who taught me how to write about love, unselfconsciously. Jim Harrison, who taught me how to write about nature and the self as one. Gwendolyn Brooks, who taught me that poetry is storytelling and beautiful language is to be mastered with technical form. Albert Goldbarth, who taught me how to write from the *feeling* part of the intellect. Crystal Good, who taught me that writing from the West Virginian perspective is a gift. Osip Mandelstam, who taught me that poetry must examine one's society honestly. Langston Hughes, who taught me that beauty, power, and complexity can be contained in one word, one line, the briefest of verse. Walt Whitman, who taught me that when in doubt, return to the land, our shared natural essence, to seek truth.

There are countless other poets and writers who left a visible imprint on my writing. I never took a poetry writing class, so the bookstore was a classroom. There are three poets in particular who have most profoundly influenced my style and affected my worldview.

Wisława Szymborska, the great Polish poet. I will forever strive to be as wise a woman and poet as Szymborska. Her poems have taught me that humanity is most easily excavated when one delves into the smallest bits of life. "In Praise of Thought," the poem for which this collection was named, was inspired by Szymborska's "In Praise of Dreams." I dedicate my poem to her eternal memory.

Khalil Gibran, the great Lebanese poet. As a young child of mixed roots, my Middle Eastern ancestry was the most called upon, externally and within. There were two copies of *The Prophet* in my home. Before I knew what poetry was or could be, I had read the words of *The Prophet*. I had a primordial desire to know the work and be proud of its meaning because Khalil Gibran was *"Lebanese like us!"* Beyond his verse, Gibran provided me with a depth of wisdom that shaped my personhood.

Mariah Carey, the great American poet of song. I lovingly borrowed from her profound lyricism in "Ode to Mariah." Her music defined my adolescence, soothed childhood wounds, taught me that language and melody can be tonic. She is a distinct lover of language; I would often run to get the dictionary after listening to a new album. She's like honey! I am forever a lamb.

I am incredibly grateful to Shoshana Zuboff for enlightening me through her work *The Age of Surveillance Capitalism*. I have grown immensely in understanding of the internet, capitalism, and society through her writing. I implore every human to read this book.

And to all of the beautiful connections I hold dear in this life; there is no life without another.

To my dear Simone, my longtime number-one (and only!) fan. You have been a steadfast champion of my poetry, a safe space to share my work. We share a language and a sister heart.

To the designer of this book, Visnja Brdar, for capturing the essence of my thoughts in line and color. You brought this manuscript into stunning form. You are a true artist and I remain grateful for our most kismet introduction! I love collaborating with you in friendship and design.

To my love, Christopher. Thank you for loving, listening, supporting, and making me feel special and alive. Thank you for being present with me unconditionally. I'd be lost inside my mind without you. You draw me out with love.

To my dear family, especially Debbie (a mother *and* a writer!), Lauren, Francois, Lola, and Max (a nephew *and* a writer!). And friends who allowed me to be poetic, a writer, and myself. Thank you! I hope I can return the same grace to you.

This book of poems is dedicated to Larry. You taught me the power of words, as a man of very few, by always saying: *I understand. Sometimes I feel like that too.*

Elizabeth Haddad

The
Author

Elizabeth Haddad is a West Virginia-raised, New York City–based writer. She attended Fordham University, where she studied art history. In 2010, she created The Coffee Experiment, a website of essays and photographs that explored people, culture, and travel through the lens of a universal ritual: coffee. *In Praise of Thought* is her debut collection of poems.

Haddad Books
elizabethhaddad.com

First Edition
© 2021 Haddad Books

Hardcover ISBN: 978-1-7361540-0-7
Paperback ISBN: 978-1-7361540-1-4

Creative Direction and Book Design: Visnja Brdar, Brdar.com
Cover Design: Visnja Brdar, Brdar.com
Cover Photos: Micaela Rossato
Proofreading: Kim Bookless
Consulting: The Cadence Group

Excerpts from songs quoted in the poem "Ode to Mariah" are used for purposes of commentary and include the following:

"Melt Away" by Mariah Carey and Kenneth B. Edmonds. © 1995.
Sony/ATV Music Publishing LLC, Universal Music Publishing Group.

"Fourth of July" by Mariah Carey and Walter Afanasieff. © 1997.
Kobalt Music Copyrights Sarl and Sony/ATV Tunes, LLC.

"Fantasy (Remix) (Mariah Carey ft. ODB)" by Mariah Carey, Adrian Belew, Christopher Frantz, Dave Hall, Steven JC Stanley, and Martina Weymouth. © 1995. Metered Music, Inc. and Stone Jam Publishing, Inc.

"Breakdown" by Mariah Carey, Anthony Henderson, Steven Aaron Jordan, and Charles Scruggs. © 1997. EMI April Music, Inc. and Steven A. Jordan Music, Inc.

"Outside" by Mariah Carey and Walter Afanasieff. © 1997.
Kobalt Music Copyrights Sarl and Sony/ATV Tunes, LLC.

"Close My Eyes" by Mariah Carey and Walter Afanasieff. © 1997.
Kobalt Music Copyrights Sarl and Sony/ATV Tunes, LLC.

"Looking In" by Mariah Carey and Walter Afanasieff. © 1995.
Kobalt Music Copyrights Sarl, Sony/ATV Tunes, LLC, and Tamal Vista Music.